Critical Response to Lyn Lifshin

"Every subculture has its hierarchy of heroes and heroines. The poetry subculture is no exception. Five years ago, it was not uncommon for young poets, male and female, to be hypnotized by a photo on the back of a book of Lyn Lifshin's poems. With good reason; Lifshin was one of the very few poets who looked like what they wrote like. All the great dark sensuousness of her lines was also in her portrait. The great dark eyes batted and a generation of young poets held its breath. Her cerebellum seemed never out of touch with her loins or vice versa."

--The St. Paul Dispatch

"An underground poet with a growing following, Lifshin has a general appeal reminiscent of the younger Erica Jong. The bright heroine of her own life, casual as her poems are on the surface, Lifshin can be a sharp and wry social critic, ruthless in her spearing of hypocrites and small minds."   *--Publishers Weekly*

"Magnificently crafted poems, terse as needlework."   *--Choice*

"These poems evoke in fantasy, but with a lot of anthropological detail . . . . Lifshin's chipped line takes on a chantlike undertone, as of Native voices themselves singing from the beyond."   *-- New York Times Book Review*

"Her poems come on like a stack of Cannonball Adderly records -- blowing cool, blowing hot, sometimes lyrical and sweet, sometimes hard bop, terse and tough."

--December Magazine

"In sometimes fierce, uncompromising language, the young poet tells what it means to be a woman in time present. . . . An important addition for all libraries where poetry is important. Libraries are advised to get this book before it becomes a collector's item."   *--Library Journal*

"One of the most widely published and least understood poets on the American scene today. It's difficult to find a magazine where she hasn't been published. . . . But the backbone of Lifshin's work, those 'hidden' volumes that she's published over the years (all out of print and never widely distributed in the first place because of the very nature of literary press distribution) are a whole other type of work -- profound, historical, literary, really mainstream American poetry in the tradition of an Eliot, a Pound or a Plath."   *--Lyn Lifshin: A Critical Study*

NOT MADE OF GLASS
Lyn Lifshin Poems 1968-1989

NOT MADE OF GLASS
Lyn Lifshin Poems 1968-1989

Edited by Mary Ann Lynch

Preface and Film Journal by Mary Ann Lynch
Notes by Lyn Lifshin
Introduction by Laura Chester
Afterword by Tony Moffeit

KARISTA EDITIONS
New York

Some of these poems previously appeared in:

Books by Lyn Lifshin:
Black Apples (Crossing Press, 1970, 2nd Edition 1973, 2nd Enlarged Edition 1979)
Crazy Arms (Omnation Press, 1977)
Glass (Morgan Press, 1978)
Kiss the Skin Off (Cherry Valley Editions, 1984)
Leaning South (Red Dust, Inc. 1977)
Madonna Who Shifts For Herself (Applezaba Press, 1983)
Naked Charm (Illuminati Press, 1984)
Offered by Owner (Natalie Slohm Associates, 1978)
Raw Opals(Illuminati Press, 1987)
Shaker House Poems (Sagarin Press 1976, Timberline Press1976)
The Old House On the Croton (Shameless Hussy Press, 1973)
Upstate Madonna(Crossing Press, 1975)
Why Is This House Dissolving (Open Skull Press, 1968)

Magazines:
Caliban 1988, *Calyx* 1988, *Ms* 1984, *New York Quarterly* 1989, *Ploughshares* 1988.

A Karista Edition, published by Combinations Press, 6 Middle Grove Road, Greenfield Center, New York 12833.

Manufactured in the United States of America

Library of Congress Cataloging-in-Publication Data

Lifshin, Lyn
    Not made of glass: lyn lifshin poems 1968-1989 / by Lyn Lifshin; edited by Mary Ann Lynch; preface by Mary Ann Lynch; introduction by Laura Chester; notes by Lyn Lifshin; afterword by Tony Moffeit; film journal by Mary Ann Lynch.
    p.   cm.
    ISBN 0-918670-02-0. - - ISBN 0-918670-01-2 (pbk.)
    I. Lynch, Mary Ann.   II. Title.
PS3562. I4537N68   1989
811'.54 - - dc20   89-23934
                                                                                    CIP

Layout and design by Jack Lynch
First Edition November 1989

THINGS A WOMAN UNDER GLASS
DOESN'T GET

not much windburn
no warm fingers
on her back no
scabies no cat
scratches on her
chin she doesn't
have to take the
pill   if the glass
is thick enough
she won't hear
people yelling or
if she does it
sounds years a
way and under
water   a woman
under glass won't
be eaten won't need
to douche have
her belly stretched
by babies   she
won't feel july
in her hair smell
lilacs when it's
raining: she's like
a bug in amber

Lyn Lifshin

Contents

Delicate Machines

Heavy Love

PREFACE

by Mary Ann Lynch

One night I walked late along Broadway on my way to the F train. I was in the thick of postproduction on my film about Lyn Lifshin, two years into the project with another three to go, though if anyone had told me then, in 1986, that it would be 1989 before the film would actually be completed, I would not have believed it. But independent film has a way of happening over a very, very long period of time, mainly, of course, because the filmmaker spends most of the time coming up with the money.

Knowing that Orson Welles spent eleven years trying, without success, to get a film made, or that even people like John Sayles spend 90% of their time fundraising doesn't make the process any more bearable, or make it any easier to avoid the trap of obsession, a complete and total absorption in the film to the point that you lose track of time, your larger career goals, your dwindling, and probably minus, finances, while on the path of getting that film done. I was obsessed with this film about Lyn Lifshin and in the middle of trying to figure out what poetry to match with a wintry, moody sequence filmed at Yaddo in Upstate New York in March of 1984 when it had unexpectedly snowed and our camera equipment had frozen.

It had been a good, if frustrating, evening editing, one in which a man visiting his daughter in our basement NYU editing digs had stopped and hung over my shoulder watching, listening to Lyn's voice coming out of the editing machine, as I went over and over the same section, trying to get the sound track — Lyn reading a poem in voiceover — to fall exactly where I wanted it. "Who *is* that incredible voice?" he had asked.

It started, subtly, quietly, on Broadway and continued, picking up speed, setting its own breathless pace, as I walked down the stairs to the subway platform — a poem spinning itself out in my head. It startled me, this fullblown, seductive poem, but, unbelievably, I had nothing to write with, and neither could I find anyone with a pen or pencil I could borrow. Exhausted to the point of finding it difficult even to stay awake

1

during the fifteen minute ride to Brooklyn, I struggled to keep the poem intact, silently repeating it like a litany, rushed home, wrote it out and went to bed.

When I woke the next morning the poem was the first thing on my mind. I grabbed the notebook from the night table, afraid that I had dreamt it, that the sheet would be blank. It wasn't. I was thrilled, started reading the poem I had completely forgotten in the night save for the memory of how good it was: "You know the story . . . ." I liked this beginning. "Of the woman in a turret . . . ." Now this had a familiar ring to it, what was it? Of course, the fairy tale, a strong allusion, I liked it. "And how ivy puts its fingers across the moon."

I was dumbstruck. I do believe my mouth dropped classically open. These "fingers across the moon," this poem that had seized me on the subway, that I had dreamt about, awakened eager to recapture—this poem was one I knew only too well. It was "Dream of Ivy." It was a poem by Lyn. In fact, it was one of my favorite of Lyn's poems, a poem that to that point in time had not been published. How could I have possibly mistaken it for my own creation?

Kidnapped. My mind had been seized, invaded, taken over, and it was not a comfortable realization. For the first time I realized I had not only the usual pitfall of filmmaking to contend with— the narcoticlike addiction of the whole process— I also had Lyn herself. I remembered now her commenting during one interview something to the effect that people who spent much time with her even started sounding like her. But I hadn't expected how deeply her poems — those thousands of poems I had read as I pored over every Lifshin book and poem I could find — would enter my consciousness.

There was nothing to compare this state to but the early weeks following the birth of my first child, when I feared my psyche would never be my own again, that this flesh of my flesh would forever remain the first and often only thought in my mind. I went to sleep worrying about the newborn child, I dreamt all night long of her being stolen or lost or ravaged, I awoke to her cries and dashed anxiously to her crib when she lay unexpectedly silent, as anxiously as I had grabbed at that notebook to make sure that "my" poem still "lived."

Long past that postpartum state, I was finding my Self overtaken by another existence again. How could I trust my own creativity any more, how could I be certain that the line I would write would be my own, if I had so immersed myself in Lyn's works that I had absorbed them on some subconscious level?

I think it was about this time that this volume of poems was born. Though soon enough this fear that I had somehow lost my own creative voice to the all-engulfing Lifshin canon subsided, it had become clear to me that a certain element of possessiveness, if not need, had entered into my relationship with Lyn's work. Many of the poems that I had selected for the film, after weeks, months of reading, rereading, were poems I wanted access to, all in one place, in one book. This was a tall order, since many of them had appeared in limited edition small press publications — some of which were out-of-print — while others had never been published at all.

This collection, *Not Made of Glass, Lyn Lifshin Poems 1968-89*, is made up of all the poems included in the film *Not Made of Glass* plus a few other favorites, arranged in an order that makes sense to me. I hope it does to you, too.

Greenfield Center, New York
September 1989

Notes for *Not Made Of Glass*

Lyn Lifshin

August 13, 1989   Sunday night   after it's been raining

Last week, flying into Colorado Springs the 747 slid thru rainbows at
least eleven times and on the way to Pueblo and there at Liberty Point
rainbows were everywhere. Last night in the film *The Rainbow* based on
D.H. Lawrence's story with the same name, bands of colored light made
a wreathe around the first and last frames and poetry is like all that curve
suggests: mystery, magic, beauty, what startles, rivets, what you can't
quite reach, intangible, stunning, unexpected. It suggests a search,
transforms like colored glass beads on barrettes I started buying
obsessively this summer to pull light in, like stained glass, twist what is.

"I can't imagine any other way to be" I wrote in an answer to a
question ten days ago. Years before this I said that in the Eskimo
language, the word "to breathe" and "to make a poem" is the same one.
The two seem even more linked, even more natural and necessary than
when I first wrote that. Poems are like prayers, those s.o.s.'s, breathless,
wild, urgent, intense often as longing and you don't know who will hear,
taste or be touched by any of it.

In workshops I do exercises to develop the sensual and try to keep
my own poems earthy, direct, touchable, full of things you can smell
and taste and hear —"people yelling," "bodies crying to be taken,"
"slammed doors," "slammed glass," yelps and howls and hollerings, as
full of raw feeling as the blues.

"Details make the lie more believable" I write on any blackboard in
schools as students giggle. Later I tell them about the 26 Californians
who were sure because I wrote "Tuesday" and "Santa Cruz" that a poem
based partly on a dead poet was each of them. I've roamed thru old
houses trying to pull back women dipping candles and shivering, waiting
for news of war, from the feel of flax or the smell of damp roses and
marble.

I wanted to be an actress. Writing allows me to put on a lot of masks,
be mad girls, madonnas, circus freaks, Vietnam veterans, women in

Plymouth braiding hair wreathes, eskimos stretching caribou, stringing reindeer gut for trampolines, Indians, Holocaust sufferers and survivors, Japanese women on the day Hiroshimia was hit, bitches, sluts, nuns, strippers, doctors, carnival barkers, -- so many people in history including Jimmy Brown, Edna st Vincent Millay, Alberta Hunter and Mother Theresa. I can have lovers I might not have on the sheet of paper and get rid of what I can't.

In so many poems here, I've been able to enter into the bizarre and mysterious, trap and hold on to what could or has dissolved or might only haunt. I can be that "snow lady" or "hot woman in fox or leather" be "a woman who isn't sure where she's going but won't stop till she gets there."

I seem to do whatever I do to an extreme: I rarely dabble. When I started taking ballet, I got up to 13 classes a week. There's little in my house (except some paintings) that isn't connected to writing: a garage no car could fit in which like the cellar is overly full of musty moldy carbons, diaries whose wire spiral spines tangle and clot, little magazines from as far back as the 1960's. Posters, photographs, workshop exercises, packed up ready for new archives to live in. In my bedroom stacks of paper circle the bed, newspaper clips, scribbled verbs on wrappers, handwritten stacks of poems hot to be typed up, images on envelopes moaning to become something they still aren't yet. Lines written in rage, in loss, in joy, in longing, old torn photographs, fragments of letters I couldn't send, lips of loss, finger prints of terror, dream diaries, carbons I know I'll go back to — paper that takes up as much room as another person.

Sometimes I wonder how people who don't write or paint or sculpt or dance or compose music deal with what seems intolerably difficult, terrible or wonderful. I'm addicted to writing, even with its frustrations. Poetry makes one so much more aware of, increases, sensual appreciation, helps one discover the magical in the ordinary, gives one power, a way to shape, transform, rediscover, catch and hold and, like with dance, a way to feel alive, connected

Niskayuna, New York
August 1989

5

INTRODUCTION

Laura Chester

No, she is not made of glass, but of grit and chalk, leaves and humus, beeswax, acid, licorice and lace. Straw, feathers, tendril and hunger. She is made of flesh and word.

Lyn Lifshin and I have been in correspondence since 1969, when Geoffrey Young and I began to edit a little magazine called *Stooge*. We edited thirteen issues, and the poems of Lyn Lifshin were almost always included. That was twenty years ago, and since then the literary world has watched Lyn Lifshin continue, without cease, to read and publish and write, proving that you can be aggressive on the page and still be incredibly feminine.

I remember how Lyn would always go to excess in her submissions — she still does, it's part of her style, akin to her actual technique, snapshots from every angle. Often she'd send us thirty-to-forty poems in a long envelope, wadded in. It seemed they'd been typed in a rush, as if life itself were rushing by her, and she were moving faster than the ordinary passenger. These submissions arrived like chances thrown into the air, tossed up to be caught by her editors, readers. Always something worth reading there.

In 1974, I included Lyn in the anthology *Rising Tides*, and more recently, in *Deep Down, Cradle and All*, and *The Marriage Bed*, a trilogy of anthologies. It seems that her writing comes to fill any subject, but naturally, like rainwater. It's the replenishing energy of the relentless poet, who has not deserted her craft for another form, who has remained true to her word, her breath — almost winded with life.

In one of her letters, Lyn quoted something she'd read somewhere — "Perhaps poetry is an over-reaction to life." That stayed with me, felt accurate, and I think it struck a chord in Lyn, for we as poets do tend to go to excess, tend to exaggerate feelings only to see them more clearly.

Lyn Lifshin is truly of the excess school, even though her work on the page is trim, light of touch, almost ethereal in its spareness, as if she were just an apparition, and you could lose her if you blinked an eye.

6

We are given glimpses, turns of thoughts, pirouettes — Given poetry. And it's a rush, this language, taking — almost — too too much — in way too fast.

She is not "neat, small, expected." She is not practical, dispassionate, stingy. She is a lover, a dancer dancing on her own terms, a poet in charge of her own life. One feels that she's been almost everywhere, and that we are merely following her into these different realms — from those strange creaky New England houses inhabited by disembodied braids of hair, to the lusty Madonna sidewalk, to the sylph in the woods, free to write whatever she pleases. And I'm sure it pleases her, as it does me.

In her most recent letter, received today, she writes: "i've made my writing my life and it's given me, along with frustration, also the greatest satisfaction and joy." I can completely believe it.

Great Barrington, Massachusetts
August 1989

The Hallways Under Her Skin

JULYS IN THE ROSE LIGHT HOUSE

in the back room
where the safe is
in the back room with
a sick baby crying
my grandmother
tapping the pane
under the apple
leaves my

mother is 8   the
new doll's head
lies smashed on
the floor she is
hating her brother
spirea on the

sidewalk she is
hating her brother
and running into
the hot stove

her great grandmother
gets a cold knife my
mother screams she
is sure the knife
is a weapon

She is sure that
she's hated her
brother for
the last time

9

the great grandmother
will die without re
placing the broken
head tho she promises
this til the last
months in the
blue bed where i

will try to sleep
when my mother goes
to have my sister
and won't tho my
grandmother sings
white cliffs of
dover and the

apples are like
magic green eggs
in the rose light
behind the house

1918

a family of gypsies
comes into the store
my mother and peg
are playing in the
back of the place
in a house of shoe
boxes my grand
father dark as a
gypsy and as sly
is naturally quite
suspicious tells
the clerks to button
their eyes my mother
is dreaming of fires
and tambourines
red skirts swirling
the old woman looks
at a shoe 4 people
are watching my grand
mother comes from
behind the handbags
and corsets the
old gypsy shrugs no
everyone breathes
easy as they go but
she comes back in
15 minutes with the

shoes like a cat
with a rabbit and
she says you were
all watching me so
I had to prove I
could now they're
yours

THAT YEAR THEY MOVED IN

to the flat on the hill
something dark was moving
toward Europe my father
worked in his rich brother's
store and stopped reading
or saying much it was
so gradual my mother
didn't say a thing sat
on her side of the black
Plymouth thinking maybe
of the men she didn't
wouldn't thinking never
Rumours of war burned thru
their sleep were in the
park where you could
say something and the whisper
went to other people's
houses. Everyone wore grey.
Buildings a whole
town the color of granite
and the dim light in the
Brown Derby where they went
to drink beer that whole
spring waiting for me as
bright as warm as they'd
be for a while.

THE FORTIES

there were spiders
over the carriage
i don't remember
my mother weighed
120 had bad dreams
of war   she took
money her mother
sent for clothes
bought pots and
pans somewhere
across town my
father was flirt
ing in the brown
derby while she
read about left
overs whispered
on the round stone
bench merle doesn't
have to live like
this   heard the
words echo as loud
behind her almost
as a gun exploding

THE FORTIES

sometimes there was chocolate

in radio stories there
were always tunnels
with germans in them

even the children dreamed
what they'd do to
young girls

there were no fathers

MY MOTHER AND THE BED

no not that way she'd
say when I was 7 pulling
the bottom sheet smooth
you've got to   saying
hospital corners

I wet the bed much later
than I should, until
just writing this I
hadn't thought of
the connection

My mother would never
sleep on sheets someone
else had   I never
saw any stains on hers
though her bedroom was

a maze of powder   hair
pins   black dresses
Sometimes she brings her
own sheets to my house
carries toiletseat covers

Lyn did anybody sleep
in my   she always asks
Her sheets her hair
smells of smoke she
says the rooms here
smell funny

we drive at 3 AM
slow into Boston and
strip what looks like
two clean beds as the
sky gets light I

smooth on the form
fitted flower bottom
she redoes it

She thinks of my life
as a bed only she
can make right

HAIR

in college I wore
it up, was accused of
someone taking my
test for me

relatives were always
smoothing it down, putting
pins it it, as if it
was some strange night
beast, animal, dark
weeds to cut back

when I was six in the
cottage I'd comb it
straight in the wet
sun but it didn't
stay, it was like

fat, like my fat
thighs that looked
thin in the late
afternoon shadows

they had their fat
way in the mirror
in the damp room

tho I wanted to be
skinny with long
straight hair
dieted till

I passed out, put
Curl Free on it
and just got it
orange   as plastic
as a broom

in the 70's
people in airports
would laugh   would
sneer hippie   I
tucked it up in
to itself for in
laws   bosses
English examining
men and superintendents
knotted it tight
like a hair ball
inside a cat
a pearl waiting,
nests for some
thing inside. I

hated not being able
to let it down, hated
twisting it, twisting
myself into what was
neat, small, expected

19

I was sorry I wasn't
indian, wished that
it would grow long
enough to hold out
buildings   as if
I could climb out into
my new self that way

WAITING, THE HALLWAYS UNDER
HER SKIN THICK WITH DREAMCHILDREN

Lace grows in her eyes like
fat wedding,
she is pretty, has been baking

bisquits of linen to stuff into his mouth
all her life,

waiting for him. The hallways
under her skin are thick with dreamchildren.

Who he is hardly matters, her rooms
stay for him,

her body crying to be taken
with rings and furniture, tight behind doors

in a wave of green breath and wild rhythm,
in a bed of
lost birds and feathers,

smiling, dying

THE WAY SUN KEEPS FALLING AWAY
FROM EVERY WINDOW

This is the kind
of marriage they live in:
split and stuffed with
terrible dead furniture,
he doing anything he
can to make her
happy, saving up a
big stiff
bankroll while she drowns
in hills of carpet
wanting what she doesn't
know he's going to buy
automatic brooms
for poking
deep in all her
corners, machines to make her
panties whirl at varied
speeds and circles, bouncing
but it all stays
wrong   it isn't what
either of them wanted. Take me she wants
to scream, even on the
staircase, even in the daylight
nuzzle down my stomach
with all your tongues   but
instead she talks of oranges and lettuce
and mornings orders
rape from the milkman, boxes
thick with cream and fears each night that time of

grey teeth, that her nipples
suddenly fall like wrinkled lemons, dreams
a parade of hair and cocks, hot scrotum
marching grinding against her
in through her flannel crotch,
wild in her
vagina — balls like wet suns muscling her
flesh, great mounds of dampness, the
dream exploding birds
in all her mouths   her teeth are clogged with
sperm and feathers
and she wakes, longing, startled,
her lips pressed thin,
wondering of stains they could leave,
                    a smell of something
that is animal.
But the sheets are dryer than leaves
nothing has been
touched, the hair between their thighs stays smooth,
unruffled.
Sun falls away from every window
and a noise keeps biting under the meat of her eyes,
her throat wants something more than
glass and linen.
In closets of shoes and old guitars she
waits, is touching where he never
enters, falls lost among the lonely shoes and
                    rusty dresses,
waiting, but almost certain that they can
                    never really come to be together.

DREAM OF IVY

You know the story of
the woman in a
turret and how ivy
puts its fingers
across the moon.
And besides, no one
could hear. Ivy
that grows like
kudzu in the
deepest part of Georgia
swallowing up a
single house
in one night. I would
have lowered my long
hair to a lover
lured him with blood
in a bottle, each
drop a ruby with
a poem etched on it
or carved my initials
in the grey stone
around his heart. I'd
have talked to the
birds or waited
slept 20 years   given
away my children.
Only I was outside
trying to get in

THE I GO DOWN IN THE CELLAR DREAM
OF DARK SNOW

I don't know if it's my mother's
apartment no it's a huge old
colonial   there are two

dead women on the counter
heads sliced from their
bodies   no blood   it's as if

their heads were wrapped tight
in cellophane   if i never
go down the steps i could for

get this   slam the door   if
nobody knows i say   there's no
blood on the blue wall to wall

i call and get this prescription
put on new clothes   my husband
acts odd but that's his and

i tell him what's down there
that i want the heads
cut into smaller pieces

naturally he follows he doesn't
say   or anything back up in
the blue room full of velvet

if i could just talk to the
doctor   but my mother calls
each hour   asks if i'm

happy   i keep going to parties
but the mail gets awful
letters like warnings

i don't recognize an old
friend sitting on the sofa scream
my husband must want to kill me

the pills nothing's strong enough
to   i start screaming the dead
heads to people in the hall

i'm shaking i feel in cellophane
the same saranwrap they've got
to stop the blood is stopping

mine   i rip nail holes in it
now my prints are on those women
i never wanted trouble

don't know what the cops will
say   my husband   i just wanted
things to go on   not have him

leave   but there's ice and snow
slamming all night   each day's
an iceberg   no one knows

the rest   the terrible cold
down under   something they
can't begin to imagine

GLASS

oh I was
wrong all that
time thinking i had the
glass tree inside
me   wanting to
slice it out before
splinters tore me
apart   i
thought i could
feel the crystal
branches press
holes from
inside

do you know what
it's like to feel
that brittle

glass words
broke in my
mouth like that
boat on my
grandmother's
piano full of
bright beads
when it
spilled   worms
slid out

i expected to
be that breakable
growing hard
something pressed inside
so long it crystallizes

I was waiting for the
edges to
crack thru my
skin

and i wanted to be
soft   to melt a
lump of
snow in your
bed   water that
slid against
your hips

for years i woke up
imagining my
face froze
I didn't understand
what comes from
living with a man who
can't get inside

i opened and the
cracks filled
with ice

glass was all he could
give   expensive
glass rings
that might
cut my blood
forever,
2 clots
on a finger

my thighs
were a glass
wishbone

but i
was lucky he
pulled out

that night
tho i
slammed glass
until my face bled

red glass all over
the floor

the glass that
actually turned out
to be
his heart
was unbreakable
of course

being a scientist
and really a
practical man

THE NO MORE APOLOGIZING THE NO MORE LITTLE LAUGHING BLUES

apologizing for going to
school instead of having
a job that made money
or babies

pretending i took the bus
to an office   paper
clips in my ears
and never that i was
reading wyatt
writing my own dreams
in the dust under the

apologizing for my
hair   wild gypsy
hair that fell out of
every clip   the way the
life i started dreaming
of did   apologizing for
the cats

you know if someone said my skirt
was too short   well i explained
or said sorry   but never that
i finally loved my legs

i spent years apologizing for not
having babies   laughing
when someone pulled
a baby gerber jar out
of the closet and held it in
front of my eyes like
it was some damn cross or a star

i should have thrown that
thru the glass   i didn't
need to explain the music that
i liked   one friend said that's
noise   another said isn't denim for

children   well i laughed   the apologizing
oh i don't want no trouble laugh
over the years pretending to cook
pretending to like babying
my husband

the only place i said what i meant
was in poems   that green was like some
huge forbidden flower until it grew so
big it couldn't even fit in the house
pulled me out a window
with it toward colorado

i apologized for being what
they thought a woman was by being
flattered when someone said
you write like a man and for

not being what they thought
a woman   for the cats and leaves
instead of booties   for the poems

when someone said well how much
do you get paid you know i pretended
pretended pretended   i
couldn't stop trying to please

the A the star the good girl
on the forehead   you know the spanking
clean it haunted half my life
but the poems had their own life

and mine finally followed
where the poems were growing
warm paper skin growing
finally in my real bed
until the room stopped spinning for
good the way it used to when i dressed
up in suits and hairspray

pretending to be all those things i
wasn't: teacher   good girl   lady
wife   i was writing about cocks and
hair for years before i'd felt
when i was still making love just on
the sheets of paper

well when the poems first came
out one woman i drove to school with
said i can't take this   another said
i don't know   this can't be the you
i know   so brutal   violent
which is the real

the man i was with moved to
the other side of the bed
this was worse than not having
babies his mother said they
always knew i was odd

my clothes my hair
the books I brought to bed
they said i never seemed like
one of them

my own family they thought it was
ok but couldn't i write of things that
were pleasant   they wanted to know how much
i got paid and why i didn't write for
the atlantic

look i still have trouble saying
no   i want most of you to
like what i'm thinking
to want my hair

it's true i put a no smoking sign up
on the door but twice i have
gotten out ashtrays

but i have stopped being grateful   to
be asked to read
or to have a hard
cock inside me

it's still not easy to get off the
phone tell a young stoned poet
it's a bore to lie with the
phone in my ear like a
cold rock while he goes on
about the evils of money,
charging it to my phone

now when i hear myself laughing
the apologizing laugh i know what
swallowing those black seeds can
do   i spit them out   like tobacco
(something men could always
do)   nothing good grows from the
i'm sorry sorry   only those dark
branches that will get you from inside

Mad Madonnas

PEDESTAL MADONNA

he puts her up
on a pedestal
and she goes
down on it

NON RETURNABLE BOTTLE MADONNA

when she's cold
and glistens all
men want her
hold her greedy
in their hands
their mouths
parched and ready

she goes
down good
tastes right,
pleases

but if the men
don't have to
pay they don't
care what
happens   throw

her out   leave
her abandoned
on some back
road, trash

MINESTRONE MADONNA

cuts you in
to little pieces
and lets you boil
in your own juice

BLOOD RED NAIL POLISH MADONNA

she covers up
is hard   glassy
and bold, a
little chippy

MADONNA OF HER SELF

people try to
take her
house her cat
her car to
make her poems
something different
her mother wants
her ritalin and
men to throw down
the toilet   phones
ring all night
someone wants her
to write a blurb
buy light bulbs
do freebies   i saw
yr face i want your
everything but
she sleeps curled
at night alone
an apostrophe
trying to know
she has to
posssess her
self first

MADONNA WHO WRITES TEN POEMS A DAY

as if the poems were
vitamins she spits
out instead of
swallowing   one poem
gets the blue out
of her   calms like
vitamin B   another
heals   makes for
good sex supposedly
others make bones
and muscles
stronger   cure
night blindness
protect   grow hair

THE MAD GIRL REMEMBERS
JFK'S ELECTION 25 YEARS AGO

curled in a grey chair
as if the floppy pillows
were her own arm,
that January, a fist
of herself as Robert
Frost's hair fell
against his eyes like
corn tassell and the
light and snow made
it hard to read as
she finds menus
written in red in
candle lit bars.
Cars were skidding
on Main Street her
sister ankle deep
in Washington DC
mud in a pink even
ing gown of taffeta
hanging on the shower
of the Hilton Hotel
before she'd be
flattened among the
dancers cramming to
see Kennedy and if
Jackie really was as
thin as in Vermont

grey moved in close,
slid over Piers
Plowman and Beowulf
as she wondered how
she could melt this
ice, making a moat
around her as she
still does

THE MAD GIRL FINDS "BORING SHOT IN THE FIFTH WITH COLORS"

on the sliver of paper
stuffed in her bag,
photographs of children
at her 6th birthday
party   a whole world
that's slid from her hands.
"colors of" graze her
forehead like the car's
mirror when the Oldsmobile
entered her from behind,
not the guava and mauve
dream light they wouldn't
use for the film. She
watches as the leaded
plum greens under where
late April snow couldn't
reach, like hope in a room
two sleeping people 35 years to
gether wake up in, thinking
ahead, moaning into some
brown sofa's wool "there
must be more." Or was it
"Carlos" not "colors"
Carlos from the torn lathe
and smoothed down cherry
in the house the man who
wanted to raise strawberries

and babies lured her to,
wild for her too, wild
for her eyes and her
leaded Tiffany windows,
pale   out of her touch
now as a body lying
on the bottom of a lake
she could remember
white and smooth,
the news of the accident
never reaching him

THE WOMAN WITH A

dead cat   the
woman with moon
dust in a safe
deposit box the
woman who had
no children had
a husband then a
boyfriend like a
child the woman
who bought too
many clothes the
woman carrying
wood back to the
car   tripping
on branches in
a field of ruined
apples woman
with a reputation
for being some
snow lady or
hot woman in a
fox and leather
foxy woman woman
with a pad of
paper under her
skin in love
with hating
waking up with
snow in the bed

trying to write
yes in it write
it will be on
the crust ok
ok tho her
fingers burn

A WOMAN IN A CAR DRIVING

downstate   letting
leaves burn into
her the wipers
scrape so a woman
on a road that
seems to go on
a woman who keeps
too many men sure
most will leave
a woman with
papers a woman
with a reputation
a marked down woman
looking for exits
pushing down on
the gas too far

she is at the edge
of   she is so
tired a woman whose
life feels like
a drop of mercury
a woman whose cat
is dying a woman
with a manuscript
no one will eat
a woman whose
mother cares too
much a woman in
a house with no
light a woman
with a crazy
husband a woman
who isn't sure
where she's going
who still won't
stop till she
gets there

TEXAS RANCH

"I'd say this bull was killed
for research"

She drove her 79 Chevy pickup
west from Laguna Vista
slithered its metal cheek
to cheek with a rusted
Ford truck but didn't
get out, just lowered
the window slow as an
eyelid. Her skin glowed
in the moon like a
Texas cheerleader named
Ivory Baby in 1976 but
her tongue didn't stop
and her lips sucked him
dazed past the ripped
up fender. Later in the
town's one bar he wondered
what there was to do in
these parts   "could give
you the lowdown" she flicked
in his ears, got out her
keys 12 miles from there
shoving him off her   she
slid out of her seat into
a circle of lowered lights
a cat howled and she yelped
with it. Other women came,

their teeth gleaming like
knives leading a dark
animal. He thought he'd
leave, but she had the
keys, could barely get
the visor down between him
and the moaning when he
saw her take something
long and dripping toward
the v of her jeans
turning the blue purple,
staining herself as if
she'd given birth

IN SPITE OF HIS DANGLING PRONOUN

He was really her favorite
student dark and just
back from the army with
hot olive eyes, telling her of
bars and the first
time he got a piece of
ass in Greece or was it
Italy and drunk on some strange
wine and she thought
in spite of his dangling
pronoun (being twenty four
and never screwed but in her
soft nougat thighs) that he
would be a
lovely experience.
So she shaved her legs up high
and when he came
talking of footnotes she
locked him tight in her
snug black file cabinet where
she fed him twice a day and
hardly anyone noticed
how they lived among bluebooks
in the windowless office
rarely coming up for sun or the
change in his pronoun or the
rusty creaking chair
or that many years later
they were still going to town in
novels she never had time to finish

THE MIDWEST IS FULL OF VIBRATORS

you don't see them right off,
kind of the way grass ripples
in the prairie and you know
something's moving and then
it stops and starts again

love in the flat lands
matters more   the sky is
so huge it swallows,
claustrophobic as a
giant diaphragm

in the midwest they
think the east is smirking.
I could curl up for years
in a drawer where those
vibrators are kept

under flannel   waiting
for a tongue to spin
me smooth   take me out of
my razzle dazzle New York
clothes   somebody who

wouldn't say much
or talk fast and nervously
as I do   someone slow
and hypnotic as an
Indiana tornado

EATING THE RAIN UP

grey tuesday
rain all
night
you said do you
    want to go
        for cigarettes
            do you want to

        listen
    i've got a
    room we
        could
i've got something i want
you
    at least
we could
    talk

        tell me your name

books fell across the bed
your mustache
        was the kind, i
      wrapped your mouth
   into me
      yes i knew
    your thighs would be
  friendly, your
hair closing
    down

small hands a pillow

and the
wetness we grasped
that warm together

ate the rain up

Delicate Machines

NORTH/ 3

her sewing basket
from the webbed
foot of a bird

tiny bone needles
she is sewing human
hair to the doll's
skin   waiting

stuffs her
shoes with dried
grass   listens
for shells from
the sled

lifts her
baby from a bark
cradle   straps him
to her warm skin

the child swims near
her breasts under
the parka   will
never be slapped
his soul that of
a dead relative
who could easily

be insulted   might
leave its new
body   suck the
baby back in
to cold nothing

NORTH/ 51

the old often
changed their
names to bring
summer into
their bodies

they left warm
blood in the
snow for the
soul in animals
bones, teeth

they left
clams or
quartz crystals
on a hill shaped
like a man's
face so the
earth's soul might
be touched
by sun

ARIZONA RUINS

1.

Past Mogollon River
    the limestone ruins
scrape it with your finger
    and the floor breaks
      the talc
    must have dusted
    their dark
bodies as they squatted on these
    floors grinding
mesquite and creosote

No one knows
    where they went
  from the cliffs
with their
    earthjars and sandals

Or if they
cursed the
  desert moon
    as they wrapped
their dead
  babies
    in bright cloth
    and jewels

2.

Now cliff swallows
    nest in the mud
    where the Sinaqua
    lived
    until water ran out

High in these white cliffs
        weaving yucca and cotton
    How many nights did they
    listen for cougar
as they pressed the wet
      rust clay
        into bowls

   that they walked
200 miles to trade in Phoenix
   before it was time to leave

     40 years
    before Columbus

3.

Noon in the
caves

it is summer the
children are sleeping

The women
listen to a story
one of them has heard
of an ocean

deerflesh dries in the sun

they braid
willow stems
and don't look up

When she
is done
they are all
stoned on what could come
from such water

It is cool and dark
inside here

this was the place

4.

The others
have gone to find
salt and red

stones for earrings

the children
climb down to
look for lizards
and nuts he

takes the girl he
wants
for the first time

her blood cakes
on the white chalky floor
her thighs
will make a bracelet
in his head

5.

Desert bees
fall thru the wind
over the pueblos
velvet ash and barberry

They still find
bodies
buried in the wall
a child's bones
wrapped in yucca leaves
and cotton

Bats fly thru these
ruins now
scrape the charred
walls white

the people left
the debris of their lives here
arrows, dung
and were buried
with the bright
turquoise they loved
sometimes carved
into animals and birds

WOMEN EARLY PLYMOUTH

borning room   hot
fire   smoke   the
aphids on a bar
berry branch. Held
down she dreams be
comes that indian
girl dancing for
sailors. Damp
leaves   guitars
The other women
enemies now huge
mouths   claws   The
blood room spinning
Barley and violets
on her lips. Who
says the crime
for bastardy   She
sees the baby
crushed between
two other children
not hers   Screams
Chickens scratch his
face from her
She swallows his name

WOMEN, EARLY PLYMOUTH

blue herons

wind ruffling the water

snow   boots   a
cracking in the trees
the time to think of
shipwrecks   blood

not what could flower
from the cold oaks

Deer swim thru icy salt
marshes   and the women
walking with bibles
close to their skin
shiver for this too

THE OLD HOUSE: PLYMOUTH / 14

this man
had 9 children

small dress
belonged to one
who would never
grow out of it

other lips
turning to
ice   he

came back from
the wharf   shells
in his hand

sank in the white
and gold bed

white pulled across
them both like a
mist they hoped
wouldn't burn away

lying under the white
lace listening to
the baby breathing

the air heavy with
salt and roses

she chews dill
for more milk

sprinkles rose
petals in the
damp sheets

the man beside
her touches the
cradle of her
hips as the

moon rolls in
her face is like
something that

glows with its
own light

THE OLD HOUSE ON THE CROTON / 5

that first summer

so little time   philip
planting apples   building
sawmills grist
mills   coming
back from the kilns
clay on his fingers
just one child

the nights went so fast

listening to horses on the
albany post road

thinking of a second
child   grass

lilac, bees

joanna tracing
yellow bricks   ship
ballasts from europe

her father's stories of
english castles,
balls drifting
in with the

fog the
blown crystal he
gave her wrapped
in leaves, straw

thru iris   peonies   daisies
the first room in the
old house   300 years

antlers on a wall
faded velvet
faces of governors

near the fire

some man sitting at this

desk   shrubs covered
with snow not

sure how much to say
on paper about
the british

thinks of his daughter's man

lavender spice box
from a cousin dying
in essex   shoves

it in a drawer gulps
the hot wine

Even his skin
smells like smoke

THE OLD HOUSE ON THE CROTON /16

smell of beeswax, acid

children coring apples in
the roots of a black locust

september

women sitting for hours

dipping braided string

40 times for a candle

wax stalactites
growing

like the stories

that woman
travelling alone

something that happened on
the ferry running
from boston

other stories from boston

until wax coats the
bricks, shoes
their voices

SHAKER HOUSE POEMS / 11

women counted

hoed and shovelled
snow   made the rules

One sister could turn
3 thousand times and
not get dizzy   the

next morning dig as
many potatoes as a man

hammers crashing
the hot forge

scream of horses

when i
first came
he says to the
stranger pulling
the leather gently

i didn't know it
wouldn't be
just for the day

their strange clothes,
ways   but the

air was so clear
and i started
seeing things

it's been
50 years

SHAKER HOUSE POEMS / 26

lives like their
chairs   simple
functional

a taste for
primary colors
for using
pieces

living like wheels in
a delicate machine
they loved

ROSE DEVORAH

dreams of old houses
in Russia, licorice hair
fire licks as lace is
scorched, turns ash
before the wedding
and the bride's bones
are dust in the
rose light green
is sucked from as sun
sets in the after
noon. Some unknown
aunt she could have
been named for maybe
wild, intense as rare
tea roses or Rashmi
Rose incense burnt in
a room the walls
pulled from floats
thru frames that are
like mirrors, her
raw cheeks like
cherries in the rain
or blood from a wild
deer running, turning
snow color of plums

ALBERTA HUNTER

long gold hoops flashing
eyes flashing   hands
on her hips   nothing
on her isn't moving
"gonna lay it on
you"   born in
Memphis   here got a
nickel for bread   put
it on the sidewalk
went to Chicago
"never knew my kisses
meant so much"   never
dreamed life had so
She's 85   laying it
on you   dancing
belting it
her hair pulled
straight back   not
to miss anything

GEORGIA O'KEEFE

I loved Texas
light coming on the plains

huge dust storms

sometimes I'd come in I couldn't
tell it was me
except for my shape

I'd be the color of the road

Heavy Love

ARTIST COLONY THE FIRST MORNING

when you hear
him snore and fart
thru thin partitions
when his toothbrush
drips down your
towel and the soap
disappears the
toilet seat is up
each time you
use it the smell
of spam and ham ooze
under his door and
coats your clothes.
I came here
to try to escape
something, un
grounded as the
moths that licked
my eyelids all night.
His heavy footsteps
take over this poem,
black glass bead
eyes. We are
strangers stuck
facing each other
at breakfast lunch
at night sipping
wine, waiting
for someone else.
It's worse than
a marriage

COOP CITY READING

women with dyed apricot hair
say you're just like my
daughter rebelling and
she's in college too.

Love in the poems has risen
like a smoke ring on a
clear day and dissolved.
They never tasted that smoke.

I'd like a little book a
souvenir one woman in pale
blue mumbles and I begin
to feel like Plymouth Rock.

No one clapped for me as they
had for others' poems about
marriage, limoge and baby
daughters. My "Wild Women

Don't Get the Blues"
button blends with my dress
but not enough. A
man who couldn't hear

says he got what he could
out of it. Widows
eye me strangely their
red hair burns brighter

False teeth click. I
tell them that if they
thought the poems mean
they were black seeds

I must spit out, weeds
that would choke what
ever's growing. Cancer
is something I say

many think is caused
by anger that
didn't get out
blossoming, as if
that could help

POEM FOUND LISTENING IN THE PARK
TO ONE OF THE PEOPLE IN IT

everything i say you
argue with me
god damn bastard
didn't you want to
come to the park
everything i say
is wrong   i don't
care if i die
you don't know
the law   the tires
are lousy   son on a
bitch   i can't depend
on you for you can't
even pay the
rent besides i'm
smarter than you
are   jesus christ.
62 dollars to buy
a lousy   you
could lose your
life   tires like
those   everybody
i know works   lousy
lousy   sick in the
head   the tires
you're crazy   get
out   what's the
matter anyway
who's yelling
you ass hole   who

BLUE PIECES OF CHINA, SLIVER OF SPOON

sharp as the
words they spit
at each other,
leaving with as
little trace as
indians when the
rain forsakes them
Only what's broken
and pieced like
words on tape
just before the
pilot crashes
can be pieced to
gether like
words eavesdropped
Flowers grow over
where they were
as if it was
a battlefield
or a grave

EYES THAT ARE BRIGHT
BLUE AND SHINY

her natural eyes,
jade green   dancing
were lost along a
highway between Fort
Lauderdale and Boca
Raton   seven years
ago   Sharon was ten
minutes from home,
driving along a route
she took each day
when a car passed
her on the left   a
flash of light in
her side vision
she heard a pop   felt
a warm stickiness
on her face. "Instant
ly my sight was lost
forever." A 22 caliber
bullet had entered
her left temple,
destroyed both eyes,
exited on the right.
She never lost con
sciousness, managed
to ease the car to
stop along the road
honked her horn to
attract attention

when she felt a
hand touch her
shoulder she screamed
a man offered to
drive her to a
hospital but instead
took her to his apart
ment   raped her over
and over 8 hours
stabbed her in the
chest and throat
slashed her with
a knife from head
to toe   felt her
pulse   collected her
clothes   wrapped them
in a plastic bag
When he left she went
to the patio and screamed
for help   police said
the only reason she
survived was the rapist
was sure she was dead

HOW IT HAPPENED

There was this
hootch outside in
the trees. When we
came back the old
people were crying.
After that I'd shoot
up all the time the
little kids pulling
at my knees crying,
the old women had
popsicle sticks,
they were scraping
pieces of a woman
off the wall, I
could tell that by
the breasts in a
corner. Even the
animals wouldn't
come near us

*

You see a guy get his
face blown away   you
do things you don't
want to think of.
By the sixth day I was
mainlining all the

time   not to feel
high   I didn't want
to feel anything

*

First you're so
scared   then it's
hard to live with
yourself   But I
didn't get hooked
until the hospital
in Japan. You
understand they
napalmed us by
mistake. First I
couldn't feel
much. Water won't
put it out. Now
I go out in the
sun and I feel
fire. I wanted to
get off Morphine
but they said why
not try unemployment

HE SAID IT WAS OK

in that first daze
seeing my leg torn
off over there
by the tree   slow
motion   a flick   then
I'm carried over to
where the copter
should be and I feel
my other leg full
of something   reach
to touch and whole
chunks of my thigh
come off in my hand
that's when I started
getting mad, enough is
enough   what's the
story I asked the
man with the bluest
eyes   I'll always
remember and he'd
gone   gotten my
other leg, put it
under the blanket so
I won't freak. Don't
shit me man I'm
yelping I saw my
other leg on the
other side of the
trees I want to know
about the leg I still
have. They sent up

blue smoke   copters kept
spitting   finally they
loaded me on top of a
pile of the dead
blood slurped as we
started moving   bullet
casings burned my
chest. The copter so
heavy it could barely
lift up out of elephant
grass but the pilot's
eyes saying it will be,
putting a cigarette
in my lips that were so
dry they couldn't ask
if what was left could
still get me into trouble

I REMEMBER HAIFA BEING LOVELY BUT

there were snakes in the
tent   my mother was
strong but she never
slept, was afraid of
dreaming. In Auschwitz
there was a numbness,
lull of just staying
alive. Her two babies
gassed before her, Dr.
Mengele, you know who
he is? She kept her
young sister alive
only to have her die
in her arms the night
of liberation. My mother
is big boned, but she
weighed under 80 lbs.
It was hot, I thought
the snakes lovely. No
drugs in Israel, no
food. I got pneumonia,
my mother knocked the
doctor to the floor
when they refused,
said I lost two in
the camp and if this
one dies I'll kill
myself in front of

you. I thought that
once you became a
mother, blue numbers
appeared, mysteriously,
tatooed on your arm

ADOPTING BABIES IN BANGLADESH

a woman is sorting thru
an aisle of them like picking
the nicest melon
in Shoprite

the lightest ones
go fastest

ones with both
legs here

one of two abandoned
left in a tied
up sack by their
father in the trees

the little girl bit
thru the cloth
made it to the village

a plane load of babies
in African red cloth
shipped to Denmark and Germany
their names changed
to John and Fritz

teddy bears   no gourd rattles
When something makes
them cry they
look for their old clothes

TWO SNOW AND RUST SUNDAYS

Snow, the color of
rust and wind that
scrapes the old
railroad ties

No trains
anymore, just
Sunday bells
they knock the grey
sky, smoke falling

Close to this
blurred hill
whispered and now
mostly forgotten,

Patty Bissette
strangled in Boston
that winter, a
different Sunday

gone in a scream
of blood stockings

(and whose baby
in her the
town kept wondering)

Snow and rust bless her
I lived here once too

AFTER GLIDING BACK

the stillness of pines
with only skiis slicing
the blue   and the rooster
piercing the black light
still wrapping us   even
back in the house where
our boots dripped on
sleek wood and you said
lets see if the electric
blanket still works. My
phone like a siren,
my mother signalling, ring
ing once   ringing again
then starting over.   Her
aloneness in the apart
ment she never fixed up
and won't, two doors from
where my uncles are sell
ing the stores.
My mother asks if I want,
before the doors are
nailed down, a blue vase
from Italy, towels to
match the ones I still
haven't used. Something
in her scared and wild

as an animal whose food
is being torn away, a
blanket of loss and
darkness wrapping her.
That darkness like the
ashes of someone cremated
I'm trying to scatter
over the Hudson, blow
ing back in my face

THE VISIT

Each time we come there are a few extra stairs.

We want to be tired when we get there and
sleep in the dark orchid room.

Insects eat through screens,
the closet is full of dead clothes

and David's letters.

In the morning we eat as much as we can and
talk of wars and parties, the new prints we bought
were they expensive?

Will they last?

Say something to please or to
make people laugh. Don't hurt anyone or explain.

But why does my sister stay locked
in a strange rage, alone, behind closed doors?

Bad paintings on the walls, the wood is
being eaten away

and those old plastic flowers.

Still an apple tree grows outside the apartment window
where no tree should,
tall and thin with very small green apples.

Later we go to the new shop
that was once a First National
and throw nails down over the abandoned railroad,

walk past the brick town house and
all the clapboard homes where daughters of Episcopal
ministers used to live.

Back in the high rooms
there are photographs of relatives
newly dead. A father, my father I think,
pasted on mirrors

from 1938 or 39.

And the waterfall rushes, even in
July, the creeks waters in the orchid room are

louder than crying.

We must sort things out, talk about stocks and settlements,
the divorce that was stopped by his death.

Night beetles fall upsidedown to the floor
near dusty bottles.

Later in the day we leave, put the heavy love at a distance.
These images can never be unified

or undone

AFTERWORD

Tony Moffeit

Lyn Lifshin has been a dominant figure in the world of American poetry for the past twenty years. It has been an era dominated by the poet/visionary, the poet/personality, the poet/performer, the poet/ pop culture figure, the poet/guru. Lyn has been all of these and more. It is an era that feels the ghosts of Walt Whitman, Henry Miller, and Jack Kerouac, a triad that gave us the poet as visionary, prophet, and guru. It is an era that has carried the shadows of those two huge twentieth century figures: Dylan Thomas and Federico Garcia Lorca. Their religious feel for life. Their folk rhythms. Their surrealism. Their lyricism. Their enormous personae. It is an era that is haunted by the ghosts of Sylvia Plath and d. a. levy, two early suicides by a couple of poet/visionaries that showed us how great the risk, how close the edge, how the poet can lose control. It has been an era dominated by a few individual voices rather than poetry movements: Charles Bukowski. Carolyn Forche. Gary Snyder. Diane DiPrima. And Lyn.

The first thing to know about Lyn is that she is one of the people. Like Lorca and Thomas she intermingles, attains an intimacy, brushes shoulders, becomes one with her subjects and audience. It is a folk consciousness that few poets attain. She is one of whom she writes. Yes, she wears a hundred masks. Yes, she is a recluse in Niskayuna, New York. Yes, she is an extremely complex and provocative personality. But, first of all, she is a story-teller, a tease, a friend, a person who will deal with you on a gut-level, who will laugh, and cry, and argue, and agree, and deal with you honestly. She begins with the fact that the Eskimo word for "to breathe" is the same word as "to make a poem." And, to write, for Lyn, is to breathe. She lives and breathes the word. She lives and breathes her poetry. She has become the most prolific poet in America. She has published over eighty books and appears in almost every poetry magazine published. Almost through sheer effort of will, it seems. For she is associated with no university, no poetry community, no school of poetry. And, she has only begun. She is still young for a poet and has more energy than ever. More energy for her obsessive writing, more energy for her compulsive submitting, more energy for her workshops, talks, readings, and creative collaborations. But first of all, more energy for her sharing, for her touching, in some way, the people.

It is the era of the performance poet, and Lyn is one of the best. She becomes another person in her poetry performance. In fact, she becomes other people. She takes on enormous power with her masks. She is in touch with another reality, like all great performers. She is a supreme actress who can exhibit the gutsy blues of a Janis Joplin or the sensitive painting of a Southwest landscape a la Georgia O'Keeffe or the playful sexiness of her namesake, rock star Madonna. She is at her best in her angry, rebellious Mad Girl persona. Her animal urges gravitate, and she becomes a luminous monster, beautiful to behold. Her face twists into a grotesque loveliness, and the uglier she gets, the more beautiful she gets. Her voice changes from vamp to voodoo woman, and she casts her spells with her words.

In 1984, Lyn was the recipient of the Jack Kerouac Award for her book, *Kiss The Skin Off*. It is significant that she won the Jack Kerouac Award because she has succeeded Kerouac as an innovator of style. First, she is an inheritor of the spontaneous mind in poetry that was created by Kerouac and Allen Ginsberg. In Ginsberg's words, it is "a concomitant potential of being able to breathe and to use the immediate flash material from the mind as it came up from the complete unconscious." Lyn's breathless, jazzy, stream-of-conscious style is today's best example of this lyrical surrealism called the spontaneous mind in poetry. And, perhaps her greatest stylistic gift was the dissolution of the logic of the line break in poetry. The line break became subordinate to the appearance of the poem as a whole. The line break became a product of chance and gave a new, hip, absurd, surreal feel to the modern poem. It combined beautifully with the spontaneous mind in poetry to give an extremely experimental, totally innovative approach to the modern poem.

Lyn Lifshin combines two other major stylistic forces in her poetry. The first is the narrative strain, the story with a "punch" to it, the Bukowski type of poem, the poem that is a little short story or little movie. The second is the dreamy, surreal quality, the Lorca type of poem, the stream-of-conscious, lyrical type of poem. Her best poems fuse the two elements into a surreal story that is irresistible. And, the influences of popular culture cannot be ignored. Lyn is a distant relative to Theda Bara and the vamp persona is one that emerges in her poems and her readings. There is a blues strain that goes back to her association with folk/blues artist Eric von Schmidt, who also did the art work for her volume, *Museum*, and wrote the early Bob Dylan number, "Baby, Let Me Follow You Down." The primary music she listens to is the blues and she has mentioned more than once the primal influence of the blues artists, their raw power, primitive rhythms, chant-like quality, twists of language, and spontaneous delivery.

The twentieth century has been a century of the individual in poetry. It has been a period in which the poet confronts and challenges, becomes an outsider, an outlaw. It has been a century where the poet has expressed the full range of emotions, has explored the strange, the twisted, the bizarre, the dark areas of existence. It has been a century of a wild independence. Lyn's predecessors are blues singers, Spanish gypsies, silent movie stars, Village hipsters, those who are obsessed with life, possessed with their stories, and mad to share, to touch, to connect. Her philosophy might be summed up by the words on a button which she used to wear: "Wild Women Don't Get the Blues."

This collection is the most representative of Lyn's total work. It might be subtitled "Lyn Lifshin's Greatest Hits." It contains Lyn's greatest poems, and it has been a long time coming. Editor Mary Ann Lynch has gathered together a sampling of the best of Lyn's poems and has organized them into a cohesive whole. It covers the spectrum of Lyn's major voices: the bluesy, feminist "The No More Apologizing the No More Little Laughing Blues," the Madonna persona, the Mad Girl persona, the icy, terrifying voice of being trapped in a marriage (including the "glass" poems), the mother/daughter voice, the personal, autobiographical voice of "Hair," the erotic voice of "Eating the Rain Up," and the blues voice of "Alberta Hunter." It also covers a range of subjects: the historical poems, including some *Old House On The Croton* poems and some *Shaker House* poems; a couple of Southwest poems, "Texas Ranch" and "Arizona Ruins;" a poem about a Jewish woman in a Nazi concentration camp; a Vietnam vet poem; a poem about Yaddo artists' colony; and a poem about giving a poetry reading. The volume ends with the extremely evocative "The Visit."

This collection captures the marvelous range, innovative style, and variety of voices that make Lyn Lifshin one of the most powerful forces in contemporary poetry.

Pueblo, Colorado
August 1989

99

The Film
LYN LIFSHIN: NOT MADE OF GLASS

A documentary on the awardwinning poet

LYN LIFSHIN:
NOT MADE OF GLASS

a film by Mary Ann Lynch

"Lyn is a role model for any artist"
-- Yvonne

*"She's a true poet—one who can deal in strong
shock subjects but not do it to call attention"*
-- William Packard

Since her first published poetry in the 1960's , Lyn Lifshin has written virtually nonstop, authoring more than 80 books. Now this first film portrait takes us inside the life and background of this unique American writer, going behind the scenes at Yaddo, the Caffe Lena, and in her Upstate NY home, with appearances by William Packard, Ed Sanders, Joseph Bruchac, Janice Eidus, and Yvonne. *Ideal for programs on creative writing, publishing, the small press, surviving as a writer, women's studies, the Sixties, and more. Available from Karista Films for purchase or rental in 16mm and video.*

Lyn Lifshin: Not Made of Glass. Color, sound, 16mm, 55 minutes. 1989 Release, Karista Films. Produced, directed and edited by Mary Ann Lynch. Associate Producer Jack Lynch. Director of Photography Jonathan Rho. Sound Ralph Fujiwara. Production Manager Letitia Splain Dayer. Music Gregory Alper. Assistant Camera Mark Smith, Carlos Reyna, Jack Lynch, Eric Lau. Sound Editor Mary Ellen Porto. With assistance from the Brooklyn Arts and Culture Association(BACA), Helena Rubenstein Foundation, NYU Tisch School of the Arts, Poets & Writers, Club QE2, and with the cooperation of the Caffe Lena, the Greenfield Review Literary Center, Myers Studio and Art Gallery, *Ms.* Magazine, and the Yaddo Corporation. The film is a sponsored project of Media Network.

Photograph p. 100 -- *Not Made of Glass* film crew l. to r. Mark Smith, Mary Ann Lynch, Margot Lynch, Jonathan Rho. On location at the Greenfield Literary Center. Photograph Jack Lynch

Lyn Lishin: Not Made of Glass
Film Production Journal

by Mary Ann Lynch

This brief selection from my journal offers a taste of what film production is like. Working as an independent is really not that different from working under the NYU Film School system, which is where I started *Not Made of Glass*, though by the time I finished it I was two years out of school.

The film began as my second year project at NYU Grad Film, but unlike most students who don't bring their second year film to a print, I knew from the beginning that I wanted to make a film I would complete. Unlike most of those in my class who were in their early twenties, single and starting on what would lead to their first career, I had already worked sxteen years as a teacher, writer and photographer and was at NYU getting at last the formal training in filmmaking I had always wanted. After a first year spent mastering production skills on three of my own short films and others I crewed on, I had no more time to spend making films that wouldn't have a life after NYU.

Added to the pressure of being an older graduate student I had two growing children back at my real home way Upstate who fully expected, at least at first, their mother to turn into the next Steven Spielberg. I was always thankful for the fact that my husband Jack was more realistic -- not that I didn't want to produce and direct features -- but he knew I had no expectations of being hoisted up by the old boy network into Hollywood, and that, in fact, the world of the independent filmmaker was what really appealed to me.

The more I cast about for a subject for this second year film, the more narrative scripts I began, the more I returned to thoughts of Lyn Lifshin, whom I had always thought fascinating material for a film. Though we didn't meet until I was well established, publishing my own small press journal, *Combinations, A Journal of Photography*, I admired her writing and total commitment, and after our first meeting we quickly became friends. We shared similar struggles and neuroses, over work, family, surviving as independents.

In 1983, when I started actively considering making a film about Lyn, she was as prolific as ever, almost weekly having articles written about her, books appearing one after another, giving readings in a number of states as well as in the Albany area, appearing on talk shows, early ones, afternoon ones, midnight and all-night ones -- she was everywhere, it seemed, and yet, still no one had made a film about her. In spite of the fact that I had gone to NYU specifically to learn narrative filmmaking, I decided the film about Lyn was the only one of all my ideas that had much merit. I knew she had a large, loyal, and avid following; I was fairly confident of the audience for such a film; and from my experience as an independent publisher and a renegade streak inherited from my father I wasn't afraid to tackle even independent film distribution if it came to that.

And so in the Fall of 1983 I began to prepare for the shoot, which would take place the following March. Production would continue in five subsequent shoots as I kept adding to the original material, fleshing it out with interviews with other literary figures, a special event in Albany at which Lyn was honored along with other area celebrities including William Kennedy and Maureen Stapleton, additional scenes at Yaddo, and one shoot where nothing except the photographs used in the bio section were shot. Soon a pattern developed: shoot, sync up the dailies, rough edit, go to work and earn more money, shoot, rough edit, work, work, work, shoot, and so on. The film was like a patchwork quilt endlessly stitched in stolen hours.

I can't begin to capture in these few pages the total universe of the making of this film. It is threaded with memories, of my daughter working as sound assistant, my son spreading the tripod so I could do a few pickup shots, my mother giving me an unexpected bond which immediately was turned over to partial payment of a lab bill, my husband Jack on midnight runs to train stations, post offices, picking up, sending out, returning equipment, me, whatever was needed, of Jonathan, Mark and I, a scant crew of three at the "Bring Home the Stars" event, the union man approaching in his raspy voice telling me I had no right to be filming, of the rented Steenbeck hauled up 51 stairs and sitting in my room six months as I worked nights editing after long days at Crown Publishing, the"interim" place for work that became a welcome kind of home base, of the hundreds of times people said "Is the film finished yet?" and all the times I had to answer, "No, not yet," of countless trips to and from labs, editing rooms, studios carrying boxes of film till I thought my arms would drop off, of setting up an editing room in Greenfield and renting the toobig truck to take the Steenback back to New York City, Jack and I kidding on the Tappan Zee as the machine lurched back and forth how the epitaph might read if it toppled us over the side, of that first call from an enthusiastic film programmer who had been mesmerized by the film and wanted to schedule us for an event, of Lyn's infinite patience and generosity of spirit, meeting my every request for new tapings, last minute scheduling, publicity photos, copies of books, retyped poems . . . I can't begin.

Much of this journal turns out to be about other film productions, those I was also working on as a requirement of the graduate degree program. But this split responsibility reflects the reality of filmmaking. Most filmmakers find themselves juggling three or more projects at once, the one you're finishing, the one you're starting, the two or three you're trying to get financed, a longrange script that's always in the back of your mind, and those that come along unexpectedly. In my case, I put down this documentary for nearly a year in order to finance and shoot another film, my narrative thesis at NYU, which is in fact still unfinished, waiting a final injection of funds.

And then there was the film that came along at a critical stage in my final editing of this one, a film which seemed meaningful enough -- though it didn't offer the promise of much money, at best deferred wages -- that I actually laid aside my own film for a holiday trip to the West Coast, only to be met by suspicion by two co-producers who wondered what kind of a woman would desert her family at Christmastime for the sake of a film.

No one should think the time frame over which this film was made, or the way in which it was financed -- painful bit by bit, from the first shoot in March 1984 to the final lab work in March 1989 -- represent an approach to filmmaking worth copying. Please don't. On the other hand, my way of managing a major career change, keeping a family intact, and eventually completing a 16mm, 55 minute film, should certainly offer hope to all those wanting to tackle this complex, unbelievably expensive and all too elitist medium.

For better or for worse, I have produced, directed and edited a documentary feature about a woman whose life I believe embodies the kind of fierce independence and commitment it took for me to tackle this kind of project on my own terms, in my own time. I did this, I must add, only with the solid, unwavering moral support and encouragement of my two children, Margot and Zack, who grew to adulthood in the course of these last five years, and my husband Jack, without whom there would certainly be neither a film nor this book.

Feb. 9, 1984 New York City   Carrying Lyn's words around like a solid block of concrete around my neck, my yoke of guilt always reminding me of the film to be made and the work still to be done in preparing for it. Words come so easily to Lyn and as I read her journal entries, the self-interviews, the articles on her poetry, not to mention the poetry itself, I am overwhelmed at times by the sheer volume and possibilities the work suggests. The film in my mind keeps metamorphosing and each time I read new poetry yet another approach suggests itself. March, my shooting time, is so close, now on the same calendar page as the one I'm looking at! I have to work very intensively to develop a good script and storyboard.

Feb.10   The POST headline today was "Andropov Dead," but the primary involvement of my mind is never any more with things political or with the state of the world, but rather with the little fictions we are all attempting to weave on film at NYU. It's a miracle any of us ever pull a shoot together given the multiple demands and pressure we all work under, having to take key positions on several other shoots in addition to producing and directing our own. I remember Roberta our production teacher saying during my first year here as we approached the shooting period -- "Start resting up. Get your sleep now. Eat well. You need to be in training as if you were an athlete. Shoots are tough."
    Tough wasn't the word for it. Three films back to back, with four sleepless nights in a row, two camera jams, standing in the middle of the street by the Flatiron Building holding a camera in freezing weather as cars passed by in two directions, then having my cameraman next to exhaustion by the time my shoot rolled around, so that he loaded the film backwards during one especially torturous evening of all night shooting -- more problems than I like to remember. But this is the NYU

approach, not so much trial by error as the proverbial trial by fire. Crews out totally on their own with thousands of dollars worth of 16mm equipment learning to make the crew system work.

So today, although I have my own shoot coming up in less than six weeks, I spent the day with Arthur on preproduction for his film, since I'm his Production Manager. All morning I was on the phone checking prices for equipment and reserving it and then from two to five we went to various places: Camera Mart to fill out a credit application; Movielab to pick up Jonathan's film (I go from Arthur's shoot to his); Arthur's shooting location by the FDR Drive and Manhattan Bridge to check the height of the overhanging girder to see what size ladder we will need to reach it for hanging lights. Arthur has designed a great shot with the 600mm lens which will pan from the bridge to some homeless(bums, as Arthur calls them) around a fire to his actors. Arthur plans to hire real street people, probably from Houston Street, as additional bums.

Other stops included 721 Broadway to check another location; the Mayor's Office on 57th. Street for a permit form; and to school to have the necessary letters signed certifying us as enrolled students at NYU so that we can rent equipment from the major supply houses and not have to take out our own insurance policies.

Typically, we were reprimanded every step of the way, the prevailing attitude among department assistants seeming to be that we are all yet to be toilet trained. In this busiest preproduction time, the office was unexpectedly closing early at 2:45 p.m., meaning no paperwork could be done until the following Monday. For such service we pay $8000 a year.

February 11   Things continue to go askew with my shoot -- after talking to Tom G. I'm still unsure about what to do about him and the conflict with Ed S. Tom claims to prefer my project and so I want to stand firm, but Tom also feels an allegiance to Ed. Having lost Scott as cameraman to a paying outside job I don't want to lose another crew. So much depends on tradeoffs and personality -- crews seem to come and go like gusts of wind.

Tomorrow it's up before 6 for Jonathan's shoot -- pickup time is 6:50. I hope I can sleep. Now 11:39.

Feb. 12   Second day of Jonathan's shoot in Westbury, pickup a little later at 7:55 but still I'm exhausted. I don't have a major role in this production, am handling the food, so I'm not in a high pressure position. Still it's impossible to focus on anything but the production at hand when on a live set. Home last night at 8 p.m. and then I stayed up till midnight working on the Lyn script. I kept stopping at the same point, seem to have a block. Not that a documentary can or should be completely scripted, as a narrative can, but I have to have a general plan for "must have" scenes given constraints of time and money. I don't have the luxury of just following Lyn around with a camera and burning film as some documentarians do.

Feb. 13   Called Lyn about setting a date to shoot the test since I'm having trouble scheduling a time when Jonathan can go up. She has numerous commitments and is feeling "slightly catatonic:" a journal workshop at Siena College, another at Russell Sage, the book signings at the Open Door Bookstore and Half Moon Cafe, a trip to Boston for the Progoff Workshop and more. Then there are the questions every person thinks about when facing the motion picture camera for the first time -- will there be a lot of closeups? What if my skin reacts to the lights? What should I wear? I go straight from Jonathan's shoot to Arthur's. This is a grind.

February 14   Happy Valentine's Day. Okay, so where are my candy and flowers? The final day of Jonathan's shoot. We've been shooting at the home of Rosemary C. who has her 85-year-old mother visiting and requiring some degree of attention. Each day of the shoot I had given her lunch before the crew. Today she says she'll miss me. Later as we're leaving she asked for the man in the white shirt who had "treated me like a son." She meant Scott, who had helped her up and down the stairs. Shoots are very personal and social in this way. Cast, crew, everyone involved gets to feel like family very quickly.

Arrived at school to unload equipment to find Arthur sitting in his brokendown red van directly outside NYU with his girlfriend and dog Rocky. He said he had been there since 2 P.M. -- it was now 9 P.M., and he had just figured out the problem with his van, which was loaded with the equipment for the shoot. We decided he should unload the equipment and leave it at school for the night. In the meantime I left with Eric, the cameraman, to drop off Jonathan's film at Movielab -- it always takes at least two people to make runs in NYC, one to stay with the vehicle and one to do the legwork; Nick went home to watch "Celebrity;" Jonathan and Christy drove to Allen Street; and we dropped Scott at Tia's.

February 18   Back to Arthur's production. Got to the FDR location at 4:30 after a long walk from the subway. Arthur, Carlos and Ralph were just about to go up to the Manhattan Bridge. Greg and Laurie were there as crew and Steve and Herman as actors, along with a man they had picked up in the area to play basically himself. Face windburnt, heavily bearded, he walked hunched over, with a slight limp. His name, he told me, was Richard Bradshaw, and he had formerly worked in theatre, set dressing and props. He was polite, well-spoken, intelligent. Here he was to play a street person warming himself at a fire.

Richard helped us make a fire in a large can, knowing where to find wood to start it off-- we were recreating for the film what he did every day. Carlos, down from the bridge where the panning shot had been executed, and now made up as a bum himself, stood at the can for the medium shot. As Arthur called "Action," Carlos began to sing softly, gazing into the flames and then gently stoking the ashes with a long stick. The quiet tune seemed poignantly, painfully believable . . . we became mesmerized, drawn in by the character Carlos was creating, until "Cut" was called.

To a person, we had been moved. We praised Carlos, telling him how good he was, and then, I noticed Richard. He had stayed warming himself by the fire. Behind him, rats ran across the pavement and disappeared into small holes in the piled refuse wood. As I watched him, he watched his fellow "bum," Carlos, surrounded by the crew, receiving lavish accolades and hearty pats on the back.

February 24   Haven't written in this all week. My own film is now taking all of my time and I haven't wanted to spare any. On Washington's Birthday I went to Niskayuna with Jonathan and shot the test. He's such a pleasure to work with, makes good suggestions and totally immerses himself in the project.

There are so many aspects to arranging a film shoot. Though a documentary may seem in some ways easier than a narrative -- for one thing, there's not the matter of a number of actors to direct and a script with dialogue etc. to be written -- still there's all the logistical planning of locations as well as securing equipment, arranging for transportation and feeding and housing the crew.

In the case of this film I'm also in the midst of planning a poetry reading to film for inclusion in the film. This has meant working with Poets and Writers, the Caffe Lena, and the Greenfield Literary Center, coming up with press releases and publicity, and doing a major mailing to get the audience there. I'm on top of all this but since I want this to be a real reading, I have no way off knowing how large an audience will turn up. Lyn seems to draw wherever, whenever she reads, so I just hope this will be no exception.

February 25   "Sniper Stalks Penn Station," reads THE POST. Six people shot since April and it wasn't till number six that the police revealed that the first five were done with the same gun. We're dealing with a real marksman using a very cheap gun, the profiles say. I will begin to avoid Penn Station subway stops. I look forward to the day when I can afford taxis again. For now busses and subways are the best I can do except when I'm in production then taxis, rental cars, vans, even trucks become the order of the day.

March 1   Down to the wire. Getting last minute suggestions, reactions to the shooting script. Everyone of course has a different idea. Ian says get her outside, walk her around. D'Usseau says sit her down and tape her for hours, then pull from that for your voiceover. I think this is a good idea but I can't afford to spend hours. We're set to shoot at the Caffe Lena, Yaddo, Lyn's house and the area around Niskayuna, showing her daily routine, also at a ballet class, which turns out to be another real obsession though of course it can't compare with the time she spends on poetry. The more I discuss with her what other possibilitites there are for scenes, the more it comes down to the fact that nearly everything she does except for shopping, ballet and going to movies is related to poetry.

March 8   The shoot is over and for the most went smoothly -- we

109

managed to overcome the few problems encountered. The outdoor filming at Yaddo was definitely the hardest, when the active snowfall and bitter temperatures froze the camera as well as our hands. Probably the most stressful location, though, was the Yaddo library, where our lights blew the power. Curt Harnack, Yaddo's Director, appeared suddenly, visibly and justifiably upset -- fortunately we had completed filming when the trouble occurred.

At Lyn's we had to deal with her scared cat Memento, having its skitterishness ruin a couple of takes. I felt sorry for him, but later in the shoot he calmed down enough to be included in a shot of Lyn typing. I just hope the dish of cat food we used to lure him to her side doesn't show. Apart from that, filming went well, though the air at Lyn's, affected by a faulty furnace, so bothered the crew that by Day 2 we were all wearing surgical masks. I was amazed that Lyn could face the five us with our masks on and manage to keep a straight face, and yet she did, the sign of a true professional.

The crew's reaction to Lyn was interesting. After the first day filming her at her house we went out for dinner. To a person the crew said things like, "You have to get inside, get her to drop that persona, she sounds too dramatic." They also wanted me to get her to take her hair away from her face. But what they were reacting to is Lyn, it's the way she is, the way she always speaks, and in fact I think they were uneasy with many of those aspects of her nature that draw others to her.

The reading at the Caffe Lena was a great success, with a full house for an audience, and Lyn read well. My chief frustration was being so limited in film -- most documentarians covering an event such as a reading would choose to simply let the camera run, and then select the best takes. In my case, my budget has allowed for a minimum amount of film, so our shooting ratio will be closer to three to one than the more ordinary ten or twelve to one.

Knowing when to turn the camera on and off is such a tricky matter in a documentary -- on more than one occasion I rolled film when Lyn began her intro to a poem and then had to cut it without ever filming the reading. Her introductions became too long for me to afford to film. As it turned out, I shot more film than intended at the reading, which left me short for the scenes at her house. By the final day of the shoot, we had run out of film, one of the worst possible things that can happen.

Next time I would go to even greater pains to somehow find the money to buy more film. Even if I had had the money during the shoot I couldn't have found any 16mm film to buy where we were filming--for that matter, there was virtually no 16mm equipment at all to rent anywhere in the Saratoga-Albany area. Everything we needed we brought with us, and as on most shoots, our silent prayer was always that we would have no equipment problems, and enough film to cover all the critical scenes.

March 10   I have seen the rushes and I am in a state of real depression, feel badly about a number of things. Movielab produced a terrible work print -- some of the scenes look like mud, others are very yellow, and I can tell there was a problem in development since there are actually some missing frames within takes. I'm hoping that the exposure problems will disappear with a better print, but I'm also afraid in many cases that I cut takes too soon. Can I piece together a film out of what I have? I just don't know. And the sound -- some major problems there as well.

Our landlord wants us out of this place, and soon. This news couldn't have come at a worse time, right in the middle of production. It's clear I'll have to shoot more, and even clearer that I have to get some money ahead. I am actually considering a share with another film student -- my space would be basically the living room, an area 13' x 18' which is also the path to other rooms. Am I really considering this? I have to decide by Monday, the same day I intend to take my workprint back to the lab and ask them to make a better one.

March 12   Took the workprint to Movielab today to see about the reprinting. A manager was called in and we immediately went to a back room rather like a store room where he put the film up on a high speed projector. While the print looked appreciably better than it had on the projector and Steenbeck at NYU, it still looked bad.

"Well, Mrs. Lynch," the manager said, "You are not absolutely crazy. Your concern was justified." Midway through the viewing he asked me if my husband was putting me through graduate school. "No," I answered amiably,"I'm putting myself through school and through much other grief, like dealing with ugly workprints." He agreed that Movielab would reprint the worst portions of each reel, so the trip proved worthwhile. I also feel better about the footage in general. I should remember rushes are always a letdown, and don't begin to approximate what the edited film will look like. There is a lot of beautiful footage, especially the scenes at Yaddo.

I spoke to Lyn, who has a reading on Long Island this weekend. I'd like to film her reading at a different setting, and this could be it. If I can check out the school's Bolex I'll make the trip alone and shoot it myself. She says it's strange with all of us gone -- she misses us!

March 14   I saw the camera teacher in the hall at school this afternoon and stopped him to ask a question about film. Instead of answering, he pulled me over to the bulletin board beside us and told me to sign up on his advisement sheet. Then he noticed my name on the list for next semester's camera class. "Why do you do that?" he asked. Before I could speak he continued, "Now I cannot let in other students who are camera. You see, there are only so many places."

Nowhere was it specified that his class was for potential D.P.'s only. "I can't make you take your name off the list, " he continued, addressing me like a child as was his way, "but you should not do that."

I explained that while I wasn't shooting a film, I was still interested in the course. I'd been a photographer 15 years before returning to school at NYU and had my first year shot what many agreed to be some of the best-photographed dramatic films. Though I intended to be a Director and not a D.P. I had a strong interest in camera. He repeated that the course was for cameramen and walked away.

Walking home the long stretch of Broadway tonight I thought of Lyn and her experience at SUNY during her orals, how she realized later that her anger over that rejection had probably injected new strength into her writing. I was furious about the course but had withdrawn my name from the list. I'm already waging too many battles just to survive here to subject myself to any more.

Even if I did the wrong thing in withdrawing from the camera course, I am not going to cater to any feeling of defeat, difficult as this is to do right about now. I'm completely broke and have no idea really where I'll be living next week. Though I tentatively committed to the living room space, I have real reservations about it. Right about now I feel like a very unwanted, displaced person.

112

March 16   Have been packing seven hours straight. Physically exhausted. There's a horrid movie on about a man chopping up the woman he just murdered. Very grisly sound effects as the camera moves through empty rooms. So little on television that's worth watching. So much hack and slash. Makes me think about the joke at school -- "What's the biggest problem in making an NYU film?" Answer: "Figuring out where to hide the gun." Though not all student films fit this description, many do. I remember another favorite story, the time one NYU grad film student dashed up to another who had made an especially violent film and said, "Tell me, Eric, you're so good at things like this, what are three unusual ways to kill an old woman on film?"

I even fell into the action trap with my first film, a story of stolen money and an innocent woman caught inbetween hoods who of course carried guns, and a rapist lurking in an alleyway. True, I learned something about directing with this film, but then you learn something about directing every time you do it. What I really learned with that experience is that film is not worth the effort unless you're putting on the screen a story you believe in, one that represents not only your aesthetic vision, but also your values.

March 17   I'm odd man out -- one of my roommates is moving back in with her boyfriend, and the other has found an apartment. She paid someone $850 to take over the lease, which she actually had to bid for. New York City never ceases to surprise me when it comes to housing. Just when I've heard the worst nightmarish rental story, I hear another. I spoke to Ephraim more about the place I'm considering on the Lower East Side, just a few blocks from NYU. He has lived in it since January and says that now the neighborhood is getting much better. When he moved in, the streets were filled with junkies and there was a shooting gallery right down the street.

Operation Pressure Point helped to clear the area and now he feels pretty safe. I commented on how high the rent is -- the total apartment rents for $1200, and my share for that minuscule walkthrough living room would be $550 a month. "You're the gentry," he said. Though the rent is ridiculously high, and though I can't actually afford it, Ephraim was right.

What an uncomfortable realization: people like me as much as the wealthy are responsible for landlords evicting elderly tenants, refusing to renew leases, closing up small proprietorships, and in general changing the face of the City through gentrification, so that rents can be tripled and quadrupled and tripled again. In another sense, though, I have to separate people like me from the wealthy. In the case of finding affordable decent housing in NYC, I feel as much a victim as the evicted tenant or shopkeeper.

March 18   It's later than I would like it to be --1:15 a.m. Just got back from Arthur and Teresa's wedding reception where I wound up crewing instead of being simply a guest. I arrived at the site of the reception, a large Chinese restaurant in midtown Manhattan, around 7:30 p.m. Carlos was already there but had to soon leave for Tia's shoot, so he asked me to fill in for him, and basically I was trapped, working as gaffer. Still it was an enjoyable, unforgettable evening. Laurie and I were the only non-Orientals among the probably two hundred assembled guests, many of whom spoke only Chinese, and that in itself brought a lot of attention to us.

But what must have seemed even stranger to the family and friends gathered, many from faraway Hong Kong, was that we were filming parts of the reception to include in the narrative film Arthur was shooting for his NYU production. As the DJ played popular hits, everything from "Flashdance" to Michael Jackson to Cha-cha music, Eric the cameraman, Laurie, and I wound our way through the crowd of dancers -- me holding a light as the camera rolled.

The most memorable, slightly surreal moment was certainly when Arthur staged a scene with his new bride Teresa. As a record played a song in Chinese, Teresa was to mime to the music. She was positioned in an area at the front of the room, which would in the footage make her appear as a singer in a club. Arthur stood by the camera directing the action, which primarily consisted of getting Teresa's lip movements synchronized with the music, no easy task. Teresa was neither trained as a singer or an actress, and this was, after all, her wedding reception.

But then there was another problem -- Arthur could not quite get the framing he wanted for the shot. Teresa had to be just a bit higher in the frame. After various attempts at adjusting camera, he realized that Teresa was the one needing adjustment -- her height had to be "cheated," a common method in film, usually involving placing the talent on a wooden box called an apple box, which would not appear on camera but produce the needed height. Also a standard trick used to equalize the height of short men and tall women, especially for romantic scenes. Our problem was that this shoot had scant equipment, Arthur's decision to film his own wedding reception coming rather as a last-minute decision. Nothing even vaguely resembling an apple box was in sight, and nothing else could be found except for large empty metal saki cans. The cans were not terribly strong, and neither were they completely flat when laid on the side, as was needed to produce just the right additional height. But they did indeed produce the right height. And so it was that Teresa found herself balancing her sharp spike heels on a rickety, delicately balanced brightly painted empty saki can, her new husband Arthur stopping her and starting her, saying, "No, no, no, too fast, too fast," while we shot and reshot this unusual screen debut.

April 16   I've meant to write since leaving my convenient Manhattan Broadway loft and moving into my new Brooklyn "home," but have been so busy each day as to have been not able to make myself. My life has changed so dramatically since leaving 390, it's almost hard to believe. I've left behind that cavelike existence, the long dark loft with only the two windows way at the end, the ever-present guard dogs barking on the roof, the three doors and padlocked expansion gate, "Hombres" scrawled across the bathroom door, the stoveless kitchen, the sinkless bathroom, the boxes and boxes of strange tools piled along the side walls to be visited periodically by our landlord madly seeking a certain bolt or screw, all of that I have exchanged for two floors of an apparently normal brownstone in Carroll Gardens, which I share with two other women.

I say apparently because one thing I have learned from living in the City is that things here seldom turn out to be what they first seem. But for the present, I am happy, with my own room, a back yard with space for a garden, and even such conveniences as a washer and dishwasher. I'm told this neighborhood is a safe one, have met several neighbors, a couple in back with two small children, young professional couples, and the single man upstairs who all say the same. But even feeling safe and secure, it's going to take me a while to get used to the commute to

Manhattan. Morning rush hour is probably the most dangerous circumstance I've found myself in since moving to the City. I'm surprised to find it's often the white exec types whose tempers flare most quickly. I'm finding out about commuter traffic because I've now joined that massive crowd heading for the office by 9 A.M. each morning. My money was at an alltime low and finally, in desperation, I made myself endure the typing and shorthand tests, turned my back on the fact that I have two degrees and am going for a third, and started accepting employment as an Executive Secretary. What choice do I have really, not wanting to commit to a fulltime job, and also not at this time wanting work which will really tax the creative energy I need to be putting into my film work? This way I can work when I want, and leave "the job" at the office. Besides, it's necessary since my savings have run out, to have money coming in again on a regular basis.

April 29   Whipping along Broadway in the taxi that was taking me home to Brooklyn, I recalled the year and a half I had spent living in the Tribeca area, the long, lonely walks home at night, the dirt of the streets and street people, the isolation and insulation of the loft at 390. I had just finished working 9 to 8 at Marsh and McLennan and was in a Love taxi paid for by them. The window was down and a breeze wafted through, at 8:20 we were just at the end of a long and lovely Spring day which I had seen pass out the windows, having only the few minutes' walk to the subway that morning as my active time in the open air. "It must have been nice today," I say to the cabdriver. "Unbelievable," he replies. "You look like a secretary. Are you on your way home from work?"

   "Yes," I said, and settled into going over budgets in my head, the money I needed to reshoot at least twice more, and then about my other life back in Greenfield, two teenagers, a husband, a real home that I got back to all too infrequently. I was wondering how long I'll be able to stand this masquerade existence, working as an assistant, often to people embarrassingly ill-qualified, making it difficult for me to conceal my frustrations, though I manage to -- but, then, it's not that I really have a choice anymore. Until I finish this film, and the thesis film which I'm now planning to shoot next year, and then graduate for this final time in my life, I can't move on to the next film, one that will be done the right way, with someone else's money, most certainly not with mine.

116

April 23, 1988   Greenfield Center

Patsy Cline, "Crazy, I'm crazy for feeling so lonely." The first day
after two weeks of sound editing and I'm at a loss for exactly what to do.
Mary Ellen left this morning, the film packed in six boxes, by now it's
home with her in Queens awaiting my arrival back in NYC where we'll
set up the final cutting room to get ready for the mix.
Last night at 1 A.M. I wore black cowboy boots, walked back and
forth across the front driveway as Mary Ellen held the mike low to
record the sound for those scenes where Lyn wears boots -- walking to
the post office, in the Caffe, in her living room. We had already
recorded the sound of petals being plucked from flowers, milk pouring
into a container, finger snaps for Darlene in the ballet class, and my
series of questions. Sound effects. Layering the texture of a film in
every possible way. Who would believe the work that goes into a film
but a filmmaker? Now I'm down to the effects and music tracks, as
important as the visuals, and so timeconsuming to produce.
The poem "Glass" has been retransferred and cut in again -- we spent
an hour trying to figure out exactly where each phrase should fall, my
initially viewing it and thinking it had been lined up differently from my
original cut, with the line, "My thighs were a glass wishbone"
mispositioned, thinking that it should fall exactly with the shot of Lyn
doing a ballet step. Mary Ellen pulled the old voiceover so we could
compare, only to discover I was wrong, she was right -- I had forgotten
the next line of the poem, "But I was lucky he pulled out," which in fact
is where the image should fall, the suggestion of Lyn's quickly opening
and closing legs in the shot going with the sexual allusion of this line.
Whether or not anyone will see this correlation, there is a reason for
every word falling in a certain place, and even being a frame fast or
slow can distort the impact as I intended it.

April 24   A new tape from Greg today, two new music tracks for
"Dangling Pronoun," a new "Rose Devorah" and also another "Arizona
Ruins," and all seem if not on the mark then very close. For the Rose
piece he went to a library and researched Russian music, the balalaika,
as I had suggested, and he's come up with a track which seems just right,
almost traditional. The same with "Arizona Ruins," which began as a

117

simple one note flute lyric and has evolved to something that sounds more Native American. The "Dangling Pronoun " piece too has now moved from what I described as sort of "cocktail-loungish" to something more complex, with an edge of mystery, a darker flavor that suits the tone of the poem, both seductive and also strangely threatening especially in the apparent niceness of Lyn's delivery.

April 25 I'm still getting returns from the flyer I sent out seeking nonprofit contributions. After being turned down for funding from several places and spending so much time on grant applications I wish now that I had just done something like this before, concentrated on other sources of funding. The most reliable to date of course has been my own pocketbook but it takes so long! This is definitely not the way to make a film ever again. I can't imagine giving up, but at times it seems there will never be an end to the bills. If I had been single and totally without the responsibilities of family and another life apart from filmmaking, things would have been different but then I wouldn't be who I am and making this film!

I heard from Gretta Mitchell yesterday, one of the few other family women I know involved to the degree that I am in the arts. She's in the midst of raising $200,000 for a limited edition portfolio of her photogravure prints of the Temple of Wings school in Berkeley where the Isadora Duncan style of dance is taught. I remember Gretta telling me how she used to exchange her prints for her daughters' dance lessons, and now that's evolved into this major project! Out of an offering of 50, she's already sold 25. I knew that whatever news I heard from her would be inspiring. She's one of the few people I've kept in mind as a comfort, as a role model, actually, these past years.

And now true to form, Gretta hasn't let me down. Though not able to financially contribute, she's offered to try to set up a reading and screening at the Black Oak Bookstore in Berkeley when we're ready. Also checks from the Boulevard Bookstore in Albany and the Vermont Book Shop, both interested in selling the book too; money from Belinda in Germany; a real fan of Lyn's in NYC; and a man in Oshkosh wanting to set up a special event at the Grand Opera House when the film is done. Things are stirring, after months of going against the wind I think it's finally going with me.

Acknowledgements

Karista Films and *Karista Editions* gratefully acknowledges the cooperation, support, and assistance of the following: Mimi Albert, Josie and Bernard Asato, Robert Dike Blair, Tom Butter, Rochelle Brener, Susan Brenner, Carol Bruchac, Joseph Bruchac III, Joseph E. Bruchac Jr., Marion Bruchac, Betty Brzuchac, Carol and Richard Cramer, Cate Cummings, Diane Decorah, Janice Eidus, Remigia Foy, Sarah Gould, Cheryl Grimm, Curtis Harnack, Ceil Hershman, Ione, Assemblywoman Rhoda S. Jacobs, Albert G. Jordan, Diane Kruchkow, Tuli Kupferberg, Eugene and Annette Lazarus, Kathleen Rockwell Lawrence, Stan Lazarus, Sid Lifshin, Frieda M. Lipman, Cora Lynch, Susan Magrino, Edward F. Marcelle, Marianne Marschak, Parker and Polly Mathusa, Lucy McCaffrey, Margaret McCarthy, Margaretta Mitchell, Esther Mitgang, Darlene Myers, Tom Nattell, Nick Nebel, Joyce Neimanas, Susan Parisi, William Packard, Angela Peckenpaugh, Magaly Perez, Nancy Polacek, Jerry Dillon Pratt, Ted E. F. Roberts, Kaya Sanan, Ed Sanders, Murray Savitz, Melissa Schwarz, Lewis Sellinger, Jean Sellinger, Jeanne K.S. Shaw, Charlene Shortsleeve, Lena Spencer, Mark and Betty Strauss, Belinda Subraman, Barry and Arlene Targan, Paul Tocker, Cheryl Townsend, Roger and Kris Williams, John Wolfe, Harry Xanthakos, Yvonne, Sander Zulauf *and the filmmakers*: Greg Alper, Letitia Splain Dayer, Ralph Fujiwara, Eric Lau, Wallace Lester, Jack Lynch, Margot Lynch, Zack Lynch, Mary Ellen Porto, Carlos Reyna, and Jonathan Rho; *and the following organizations:*

The Boulevard Bookstore/15 Central Avenue/Albany, NY 12210 ◆ *Brooklyn Arts and Cultural Association*/(BACA)/Brooklyn, NY ◆ *Caffe Lena*/Phila Street/Saratoga Springs, NY 12866 ◆ *Greenfield Review Literary Ctr*/2 Middle Grove Rd/Greenfield Ctr., NY 12833 ◆ *Gypsy Magazine*/Box 283/HHB 2/3 ADA/APO NY 09110 ◆ *Helena Rubenstein Foundation*/NY, NY ◆ *Impetus/ Implosion Press*/4975 Comanche Trail/Stow, Ohio 44224 ◆ *MS. Magazine*/NY, NY ◆ *Media Network*/ 121 Fulton St. 5th Floor/ NY, NY ◆ *Myers Studio & Art Gallery*/ 1020 Barrett St/ Schenectady, NY 12305 ◆ *New York Quarterly*/ PO Box 963/Old Chelsea Station/NY, NY 10113 ◆ *NYS Writers Institute*/SUNY Albany/355 Humanities/Albany, NY 12222 ◆ *NYU*/Tisch School of the Arts/ 721 Broadway/NY, NY, Grad Film faculty -- Tony Barsha, Beda Batka, Bill Daughton (in memoriam), Yuri Denysenko, Arnaud D'Usseau, Herman Engel, Eleanor Hamerow, Roberta Hodes, Ian Maitland, Ed Pryor, Fred Sadoff ◆ *Poets and Writers, Inc.*/72 Spring St./NY, NY 10012 ◆ *QE2*/ Albany's Music Showcase Club/ Central Ave./Albany, NY 12210 ◆ *Sack Gut Press*/2513 E. Webster/Milwaukee, Wisc. 53211 ◆ *Scriven Duplicating Service*/ Valley Falls, NY ◆ *Vermont Book Shop*/38 Main St./Middlebury, Vt 05753 ◆*The Yaddo Corporation*/Union Ave./ Saratoga Springs, NY 12833

For information on scheduling the film, filmmaker, and/or poet or on purchasing the film or purchasing copies of this book, contact: Karista Films, Mary Ann Lynch, P.O. Box 423, Saratoga Springs, N.Y. 12866 (518-584-4612)